An Art of Small Resurrections

Surviving the Texas Death Chamber

Walter Long

Pendle Hill Pamphlet 408

About the Author

Walter Long is a member of the Friends Meeting of Austin, which he has attended since the mid-1980s when the meeting declared itself a sanctuary for Central American refugees. The meeting has a lengthy history of advocating for matters of conscience and human rights, and it currently has a very active death penalty committee. As a criminal defense attorney, Walter has represented Texas death row inmates in state and federal habeas corpus appeals. He also founded the Texas After Violence Project (www.texasafterviolence.org), an independent oral history and human rights project designed to listen empathetically, carefully, and without judgment to people directly touched by serious violence, the criminal justice system, incarceration, and executions in Texas. The project films and transcribes their stories and then archives the stories in the University of Texas Libraries and makes them available to the public. The project seeks to foster deep listening and exchange among all Texans affected by violence so that they collaboratively may find the means to build a less violent and more just community.

Publications staff: Shirley Dodson
Pamphlet edited by Chel Avery and designed by Mary Helgesen Gabel
Requests for permission to quote or to translate should be addressed to:
Pendle Hill Publications, 338 Plush Mill Road, Wallingford, PA 19086-6023
Email: publications@pendlehill.org

ISBN 978-0-87574-408-7
August 2010

An Art of Small Resurrections

Surviving the Texas Death Chamber

A Compassionate Strategy

I am a criminal defense attorney working on death penalty appeals in Texas. As I write, someone was executed a few days ago and someone else is lined up to be executed in a few days. There are no respites, except that the state does not kill on weekends or around Christmas. Texas lags behind few nations in the number of persons it kills under judicial condemnation each year.

My mind boggles at the widespread severe trauma and anticipatory, complicated grief the death penalty spreads among those who care about the defendants. In my office, days before her son's execution, a mother went into a catatonic state. Surrounded by daughters and grandchildren, she was unreachable and unresponsive. Another mother has told me, "When my son's execution date was set, I successfully committed suicide, but the paramedics brought me back." Some years ago, I slowed my practice, doubting that I myself could emotionally survive another client's execution. I have seen colleagues go into deep depression. I have seen many friends—good lawyers—leave Texas to work in less brutal places.

I find it upsetting to be a part of a legal system designed to kill. The death penalty is indistinguishable from torture, which includes such extremely assaultive and emotionally intolerable legal punishments within its definition.[1] Moreover, the prospective orientation of death penalty law always will undermine fairness. When punishment is defined as a future achievement to be obtained by the state, government actors naturally become invested in it. This goal orientation inevitably leads prosecutors to defend unfair trials[2] and it causes courts to look past serious errors as if they were accountants told before an audit of the desired bottom line.[3] The law is intrinsically warped, and it corrupts and impoverishes the rest of the state's justice system.

Few of my fellow Texans seem to care about these things. One of the main reasons, I think, is that lawmakers and citizens identify Texas as a Christian state. Christian religion grounds the Texas death penalty, masking its violence. This has been particularly painful for me to realize as I have tried to be a Christian. I have found that the hardest place to be a death penalty opponent is in a Texas church, liberal or conservative, Roman Catholic or Protestant. Before settling into membership in a Friends meeting, I frequently would be called upon to defend myself on Sunday mornings for being a lawyer to death row inmates. In these settings, I felt not only unsupported, I was pitied and looked upon as morally or theologically inferior.

When I heard a Zen teacher say that she was attracted to Buddhism as a skillful means to conduct a life of compassion, I found myself asking: Can those of us who come from the Christian tradition primarily think of our faith as a strategy for compassionate living? Adherents to Buddhism take refuge in the Buddha by adopting a focused, compassionate practice. So, what would it mean to say that adherents to Christianity take refuge in Jesus? What is a Christian compassionate practice? Is Christianity only about adopting certain beliefs? Or, did Jesus similarly have a compassionate method? It may be an overstatement to say that, over centuries, Christians often have portrayed Jesus's principal task in life as to die in order to appease a punishing God and restore a fallen humanity. But I do not find it much of an overstatement. Debating the meaning of this traumatic sacrifice, sometimes to the point of war, Christian churches frequently have focused more on correct doctrine than on compassionate living.

However, the New Testament provides evidence that Jesus himself advocated a compassionate strategy. Born into humble circumstances, he portrayed an all-embracing "kingdom" in which no one was too small or unpopular to be recognized. He heralded a reign of unqualified love that enfolded the enemy as though he or she were kin. Jesus taught a fearlessness that was grounded in a specific discipline which, by its design, prevents the rigidity and alienation from others that precede or follow human violence. The prayer Jesus taught his followers (the "Lord's Prayer") simultaneously assumes a dialogue with God and an interconnected world of human interlocutors. By the repetition of its terms—"forgive us as we forgive those who trespass against us"— the prayer produces *revivifying* human attachment. It is an art of small resurrections. I have clung to Jesus's prayer more than any other spiritual practice in my struggle to remain emotionally regulated in the face of my state's frequent acts of homicide.

My drive to write this essay stems as much from the painful challenges of my fellow Christian friends to provide a personal *apologia* as it stems from the traumatic legal work I have done. I hope, though, that it also will be a gift to them, that they will think more deeply about what Jesus meant when he said, "Forgive them, for they do not know what they are doing" (Luke 23:34);[4] that they will be inspired by Jesus's compassionate strategy—his art of small resurrections—and will consider how we may all work together to make our community less violent and more just.

A Compassionate Wager

Christian churches have spent two millennia discussing Jesus's divinity and death. Almost all have taught that there are certain beliefs about these aspects of Jesus that perform a gate-keeping function for the kingdom of God. They have disagreed over the content of these beliefs, but generally not about the consequence of believing. Simply put, those who assent to particular beliefs about Jesus are allowed into the Christian community and are rewarded with a good afterlife; nonbelievers are not.

Jesus indeed told his disciples that they should enter through a "narrow gate" in order to avoid the "broad" way to destruction (Matt. 7:13). But I think that, in saying this, Jesus directed them toward a narrow path of living—a strategic way of being and doing—rather than toward narrow tenets of belief. The broad way was occupied by those living and dying by the sword. The narrow gate was the hard-to-find aperture of peacemaking, of bearing (or *being*) mercy toward others.

Blaise Pascal famously summarized the churches' propositions about matters of Jesus's divinity and death as a wager.[5] Pascal asserted that, although reason falls short of proving God's existence, we still should blindly bet that God exists, because by living as though God exists, we gain everything and risk nothing. If it turns out that we are right, our belief in God gains us heaven and prevents divine punishment. If it turns out that we are wrong, then our belief in God nonetheless gains us a virtuous life. With moral goodness as a guaranteed byproduct of his wager, Pascal presented what seemed to be a win-win proposition.

However, Pascal's wager really was about avoiding divine wrath—it assumes that God exists and punishes us for failing to believe (specifically, for failing to believe particular things about

Jesus). Real costs for a participant in the wager (whether right or wrong) are dwelling in the fear of a punitive God and being motivated to do good by terror. One of Pascal's implied premises is that, if God exists, God is jealous and punitive, meting out judgment based upon belief or lack of belief. Another is that the purpose of belief is nothing more than interest in self-survival.

But if Jesus's God were anything like this, why did Jesus so flagrantly transgress religious laws in favor of compassion (Luke 6:1-11)? And if Jesus believed self-survival was of primary concern, why did he tell his disciples to take no heed of future security? He chided them for worrying about clothing, food, shelter, or safety (Matt. 6:25-34). He challenged them: Are God's other creatures anxious about such things? Jesus describes God as indiscriminately nurturing. Jesus holds up this God as a model for what he tells his disciples to *do*, not believe. When the rich young man approaches him and asks how to achieve eternal life, Jesus tells him to risk himself through acts of compassion: to sell all his things, give the proceeds to the poor, and join him (Matt. 19:16-30).

Jesus instructs the disciples to reject earthly treasure and instead to invest themselves in this hidden compassionate God. If they do so, they will stop judging and they will not be fooled by false prophets who do judge, who "come in sheep's clothing but inwardly are ferocious wolves" (Matt. 7:1-5, 15). Jesus says that, by being compassionate, by being nonjudgmental, his disciples may gain by what they do a dwelling with a foundation built on stone (Matt. 7:24-27). The rain falls, the floods come, the winds blow and beat against the house built on the works of compassion. But protected by their inwardness in God, Jesus's followers are grounded and, no matter the terrible power and destructive effects of the tempest, they do not fade from being present and vital. They maintain their compassionate works in the face of the tempest.

Unlike Pascal's endorsement of our instinctive pursuit of security from death and avoidance of pain, Jesus prescribes counterintuitive risk taking. Faith is being and doing—not believing—against the odds. It looks as though Jesus would propose a contrary wager: Assuming a compassionate God has given us one solitary and special opportunity at life, what if our fears were to cause us to fail to show up?

The Loss of Compassion

Jesus said, "You have heard that it was said, 'an eye for an eye' . . . and 'hate your enemy,' but I say to you, 'love your enemies and pray for those who persecute you'" (Matt. 5:38–44). This prescribed course of action does not contain additional caveats, alterations, exceptions, or subclauses. It does not say "but you may burn, maim, deprive, belittle, execute, or send your enemies to hell, too." It is a strategy of "perfect love" that simply "drives out" the fear manifest in violence and unreasonable disputation (1 John 4:18).

Yet, the New Testament authors themselves use judgment and fear as motivators, even commonly placing hellish metaphors on Jesus's tongue. (See, for example, Matt. 5:22, 10:28, 25:41, and Mark 9:42-48.) These passages conveying divine judgment often have a jarring effect, virtually laying siege to Jesus's nonjudgmental and compassionate utterances found within the same contexts. A good example is the passage in which Jesus instructs that he is present in those who are thirsty, hungry, naked, and imprisoned (Matt. 25:31-46). A radical statement of equality and dignity, the passage nevertheless descends into damnation of persons who fail to perceive Jesus in these representatives of the "least" of humanity.

I think these vindictive passages show a failure on the part of the New Testament authors and editors to comprehend and accurately transmit Jesus's message of love for the enemy. This assertion may seem audacious and provocative. Yet, I find the messages of unqualified love and the threats of damnation to be irreconcilable.[6] Scholars have argued that the oldest and most authentic parts of the gospels are Jesus's Sermon on the Mount and the parables—exactly those passages which are consistently filled with a message of compassion.[7] My position, however, is that those passages are unique and are qualitatively incompatible with the other apocalyptic and hateful language attributed to Jesus, as well as with the retributive structure of the schema that developed to explain his violent death. I conclude that, if we are to follow Jesus, we have to choose between his pragmatic advice and the fundamentally violent sacred story about him. I think that the churches' longstanding attempt to keep both has obfuscated Jesus's message and has frustrated humanity's growth in tempering its violence.

Jesus frames a new legal rule, "you have heard that it was said . . . but I say to you," against a prevailing retributive norm in his society (which he identifies as hatred of one's enemy) and against the background of Jewish law. The Torah, the old law to which Jesus referred only in part, emphasized the tribe, teaching the love of those who were near and who were most like oneself. It instructed against the harboring of grudges and the carrying out of vengeance against "one of your people," the "neighbor" (Lev.19:18). However the Torah also required compassion for the enemy, and this is reflected in the Talmudic teachings. Moses commanded, "Do not abhor an Edomite, for he is your brother. Do not abhor an Egyptian, because you lived as an alien in his country" (Deut. 23:8). The law also stated, "If you see the donkey of someone who hates you fallen down under its load, . . . be sure you help him with it" (Exod. 23:5). Commenting on this passage, the rabbis of the Talmud instructed: "If [the animal of] a friend requires unloading, and an enemy's loading, you should first help your enemy—in order to suppress the evil inclination" (Baba Metzia 32b). One translation explains that the passage requires the letting go of all hate harbored toward the enemy (Targum Yonatan).[8]

Although the Torah records a divine preference for Israel, nowhere is there an explicit command to "hate the enemy."[9] Jesus's contributions were to recall the compassion for the enemy required in the Torah and to radically emphasize that the enemy was to be just as loved as the neighbor. He bluntly treats this as a legal shift. That was the law then; this is the law now. Love of enemy reigns now. Now there is no difference between "us" and "them." Pray for the good of those who persecute you, not for their destruction. Why? Because God's love is now and here-on-out to be understood as completely nondiscriminating (Matt. 5:43-48). The term "enemy" leaves no wiggle room to ask who may not be loved by God or who permissibly may not be loved by us. For Jesus, love of enemy means that there is no one who is not our neighbor. With Jesus's new rule, the indistinct set of non-neighbors became null.

As a consequence, when a lawyer challenged Jesus to explain "who is my neighbor" in the commandment from the Torah to "love one's neighbor as oneself," Jesus turned the question on its head. Using the parable of the Good Samaritan, Jesus explained that the "neighbor" is not defined by such qualities as same or other, near or far, friend or foe, beloved or despised. The neighbor simply is one who shows mercy to *all* others (Luke 10:37). The parable not only illustrates that a (usually culturally despised) Samaritan provided aid to a beaten man beside the road who had been ignored by the righteous. It demonstrates a further point that, when we catch ourselves asking who our neighbor is, we must turn and interrogate ourselves: Are we being neighborly—indiscriminately neighborly?

The hold of tribalism has continued to be strong, despite Jesus's clear new commandment. The drives to define the canon and to regulate beliefs, which arose in the early church and thrive today, seem always to have been about defining tribe (or "neighbors"). Those who share scripture and beliefs are distinguished from the heterodox "others," who have yet to be saved or destroyed. Pressure to group conformity encourages authoritarian attitudes which promote credulous protection of every word in the selected scriptural canon.

The death penalty sheds light on the effect that the congealing of beliefs (and formation of a "Christian" tribe) had on the compassionate practice of Christians. For scores of years, followers of Jesus were executed by the Romans for being members of an illegal religion. They understood oppression and suffering and expressed a visceral reaction against the death penalty. Athenagoras of Athens said in 176 CE that Christians could not "endure even to see a man put to death, though justly." He added that Christians could not possibly participate in executions, as they could not even "look on" at gladiator bouts without "contract[ing] guilt and pollution."[10]

The young Christian community seemed to have been guided by compassion in its treatment of all persons. Then Rome adopted Christianity as its official religion. With the consolidation of the Christian canon in the fourth century, officially determining what was and was not to be included in the Bible, came a consolidation of dogma. Roman law was joined as an ally against unorthodox beliefs, and Christians began to embrace the death penalty.[11] Their capacity to stand by and endure the suffering of others grew in proportion to their political power. Within only a few centuries, the developing institutional churches adopted an attitude of self-survival and left behind Jesus's wager of compassionate risk taking. Instead they worshiped Jesus, venerating him as earlier Romans had venerated the emperor. Thus began the entrenchment of atonement doctrines that mirror (and provide justification for) an accommodation with human violence.

All Christian atonement doctrines teach that Jesus's execution saved humanity from its own sinfulness. As developed throughout the middle ages, the reformation, and the modern church, these doctrines inevitably instruct the faithful to embrace the executioner's point of view for the sake of their own salvation. Whether they articulate the ultimate purpose of atonement as penal substitution[12] or the rescue of humanity from the clutches of the devil or sin,[13] they present God as an agent of Jesus's death and describe the death itself as a benefit of ultimate value for the believer. They all see the events of history unfolding under the guidance of God and presume that, if God is in command of history, then God is responsible for the execution of Jesus. If God also is good, the execution of Jesus is good. There is no room to say that God does not affect events or that God did an evil thing by allowing Jesus to be killed. It is asserted that God's ways are greater than ours, so we have to trust that God is a benign executioner. These doctrines address our natural anxiety over self-survival and foster social unanimity around acceptance of this primal execution, and in doing so, these beliefs allegedly promote spiritual and emotional health. But they also retard our (equally natural) compassionate response to real suffering. They erect a roadblock to the ability of believers to comprehend fully their (active and passive) responsibilities in the world's wars, pogroms, crusades, inquisitions, and executions.[14]

Beliefs about Jesus have often caused Christians to ignore one of Jesus's most salient and consistent points: that human flourishing is rooted in deliberate cultivation of friends and reconciliation with enemies. "Love your enemies" is a teaching irreconcilable with any theology that would excuse or justify their harm or their deaths in "spiritual" or real terms. It is irreconcilable, too, with any theology that would endorse a violent solution to a problem of human suffering or sinfulness.

Recoveries of Compassion

The flower of compassion planted by Jesus seems to require painstaking cultivation and has made overt appearances within movements that sometimes feel like historical footnotes—the Franciscans, the Mennonites, the Friends, the Catholic Workers. However, arguably, the bloom also has taken firm root in the Enlightenment's ongoing discoveries of human empathy and bodily integrity,[15] which have had a huge leveling effect on barriers between people and have generated widespread recognition of human equality and rights.[16] Benjamin Rush, one of our country's founders and a contemporary of the vast legal and social changes that took place in the Enlightenment period, linked the Christian traditions that promoted love with the awakening of respect for human emotions and empathy, referring to what we call empathy as "the vice-regent of the divine benevolence in our world." "Sensibility," he said, "is the sentinel of the moral faculty."[17] It is "that of God" present in that which is most profoundly human.

The Enlightenment's newfound awareness of the shared inner emotional lives of all human beings became the foundation for the rights announced in the French Declaration of the Rights of Man and Citizen and in the American Bill of Rights. These documents, in turn, inspired and grounded the Universal Declaration of Human Rights and a movement that has evolved since World War II to assure that dignity is actually afforded to *all* people, without distinction, neighbors and enemies alike. Only within the most recent century, the term *dignity* has been given a new meaning in society and law. Removed from being a solemn attribute of kings, priests, and governments, dignity now is deemed the inviolable attribute of every human being, found even and foremost in "the least" member of human society.[18] At minimum, legally, dignity means being valued as an equal person and not being treated as an object.[19]

A consensus is developing among nations that capital punishment is a preeminent example of the denial of human dignity, along with other practices recognized as abuses: murder, genocide, torture, and systemic racial discrimination. All of these actions "treat members of the human race as non-humans, as objects to be toyed with and discarded."[20] A Canadian Supreme Court Justice has described the death penalty as "not only depriv[ing] the prisoner of all vestiges of human dignity, [but as] the ultimate desecration of the individual as a human being . . . the annihilation of the very essence of human dignity."[21] The nations of Europe have abandoned the penalty as contrary to dignity.[22] Similarly the South African Constitutional Court recently barred the death penalty as a violation of dignity. One of the judges stressed that dignity is violated by all inexcusable homicides—including murder and execution—and righteous anger must be expressed against murderers by the courts, while the government also avoids sending the wrong message: "that the value of human life is variable."[23]

Jesus, an indigent Jew deprived of political and legal rights in a Roman world, understood the denial of dignity, the "nobodiness" experienced by history's oppressed.[24] By encouraging his followers always to love their enemies, Jesus asked them to recognize those who oppressed them as possessing dignity, even as that term is now coming to be understood. He therefore insured that his followers would know and retain their own dignity. Jesus essentially told his followers that the authorities could kill them, but could never turn them into nobodies. "Do not be afraid of those who kill the body but cannot kill the soul" (Matt. 10:28).

An Art of Small Resurrections

Fearless compassion prevents us from averting our gaze from realities, including the acts of cruelty and inhumanity in which we are implicated. This cruelty is excruciating to witness and to be part of. We feel despair and want to retreat. How do we remain present and responsive? Jesus has offered clues.

The willingness to embrace compassion requires one to lay aside escapes and to fully encounter the present. It prevents any selectivity in the use of human empathy and, thus, it prevents aversion of our gaze from the raw sun of ongoing human violence (one's own and that of others). Jesus's fearlessness leads to an awareness that inexorably involves reckoning with annihilation. Jesus himself discovered that his compassion delivered him to a place where he found himself feeling the stark indifference of the universe, where he cried out that he had been forsaken even by God (Matt. 27:46).

If, as Jesus affirmed, we may have a vital, inward relationship with God ("the Light Within," as Friends say, or a "divine benevolence," as Rush described it), it is urgent, for the sake of ourselves and all others within our sphere of influence, that we seek that relationship. In that relationship is the help we need to resist our temptations to flee, ignore, or rationalize our own homicidal world. But even if we conquer these temptations and are fully aware, how do we defend our continued capacity for that same vital relationship, when each senseless murder overwhelms us in grief, when every relentless state killing threatens to extinguish our hope in a nihilistic vacuum? How do we pass beyond the same despair that Jesus expressed when he cried out? If we are to respond appropriately, we must remain engaged and compassionate—absent vindictiveness—even when our hopeful prayers for mercy are repeatedly disappointed. Jesus, in teaching the Lord's Prayer to his disciples (Matt. 6:9-14), taught an art of small resurrections.

Having ordered his followers to fearlessly enter the world to proclaim the kingdom, Jesus gave them strategic tools to remain in touch with the hidden God, the source of their vitality. Most importantly, he sent them in twos, recognizing that dyads reinforce each other emotionally, morally, and spiritually. Wherever two or more are gathered, Jesus promised, *he* was present. They were never to be alone and should always (every day, every moment, wherever they went) be summoning forth their true home in God: *Your kingdom come* (Matt. 6:10). Jesus counseled that each day would have its own troubles, so his followers should conscientiously bring forth the kingdom in each day, laying aside concerns for the morrow. The prayer focuses, thus, on *this day. This day give us only what we need and help us to forgive each other*—help us to be present with each other now, today (Matt. 6:11-12).

The prayer that Jesus taught to his followers is revolutionary, because their repeated presencing of the compassionate refuge of God (the kingdom) also explicitly requires them to constantly—at this moment, in this day—work toward forgiveness of each other and their enemies, even within the darkest of human conditions. *Forgive our trespasses as we forgive those who have trespassed against us* (Matt. 6:12, Tyndale trans.). This teaching is at the heart of an art of small resurrections—what the Jewish tradition simply refers to as "turning." It is the incessant bringing to life of relationships through constant, momentary repentance: the cessation of *judgment* and simultaneously, as a direct consequence, the ending of violence. It is a pirouetting—a turning of one's cheek, a forgetfulness of one's hands in the move[25]—that steadfastly approaches the other in compassion (Matt. 5:39, 6:3).

This presencing of the kingdom in the darkest of places, this pirouetting, this art of small resurrections, never leaves the conditions it encounters, no matter how dark, the same as they were. That is not to say that inevitably Jesus's followers would make the conditions better. History is replete with the ironic results of good intentions. But each place in which they would reestablish their transcendent home would represent an opportunity for them to move the brutality of their time in history, moment by moment, in the direction of meaning-filled, loving community.

Being Wary of Predators

Jesus warned his followers that the human world was predatory. He called the religious leaders who aligned themselves with political power "vipers" (Matt. 23:33). He warned the disciples to be ready for false prophets who would appear to be docile but would possess the inner life of wolves. He said, "I am sending you out like sheep among wolves." And, then, remarkably, he added, so be like them. "Be as shrewd as snakes." Be more cunning than those who are violent. But, whatever you do, do it nonviolently. "Be as shrewd as snakes and as innocent as doves" (Matt. 10:16).

Note that Jesus did not deride false prophets merely for harboring and promoting false beliefs. He warned against them because they are *secretly violent.* He opposed them for what they really do underneath their rationalizations. The mark of false prophecy is justification of violence by deceptively declaring what Dorothee Soelle called a "righteousness standing behind the suffering."

> When you look at human suffering concretely you destroy all innocence, all neutrality, every attempt to say, "It wasn't I; there was nothing I could do; I didn't know." In the face of suffering you are either with the victim or the executioner—there is no other option. Therefore that explanation of suffering that looks away from the victim and identifies itself with a righteousness that is supposed to stand behind the suffering has already taken a step in the direction of theological sadism, which wants to understand God as the torturer.[26]

The greatest danger for Jesus's followers was not that they would be eaten by the wolves, but that they would fall in with them—that they would join the pack. Who was described as being with Satan in the wilderness when Jesus was offered the kingdoms of the world? The wild beasts (Mark 1:13). Executions are conceived and carried out by packs. For anyone involved in the process, from the governor down to media witnesses and oneself (wherever one might be), the emotional impact of an execution is inescapable, and the temptation is to self-preservation by rationalizing the state's violence through many well-traveled means of remaining within the pack.

Throughout the history of America's use of the death penalty, clergy have rationalized the violence, assisting executioners with the wager that a repentant Christian defendant will survive killing and, upon being ushered from this life, have another chance with God.[27] In places like Texas, the public often believes this, dissociating itself from the violence. Even many defendants and their families cope with their situation by accepting this belief. Thus is the state's violence veiled. When executions were public, Christian ministers delivered "execution sermons" in churches and from scaffolds, urging the crowds to reject crime so they might avoid the fate of the defendant and praising the defendant for having confessed faith, because he would shortly be sent by the state into the arms of God. About ninety years ago, when unruly crowds were causing national embarrassment, Texas moved its executions indoors, and the chaplains followed them, continuing to participate within the execution chamber.

A Texas governor sent a defendant on the way to be killed, releasing a public statement that he had prayed about his decision whether to grant clemency in the case and had decided that "judgments about the heart and soul of an individual on death row are best left to a higher authority" (i.e., God).[28] This statement appeals to the "righteousness standing behind the suffering" as an excuse or justification to cause the suffering. Just as the execution sermons did, it hides the killing as an inconsequential act compared to the encounter with God that is implied to follow. Although they do not speak, by their very presence, state prison chaplains participating in executions today continue to send these messages. However well meaning they may be as individuals, their presence provides illusory moral grounding to the state's violence.[29] The Texas death penalty would end tomorrow if chaplains would simply follow Jesus out of the execution chamber.

Origins of a Predatory Story

The protagonist in a story by Jorge Luis Borges observes that "humankind has told two stories: the story of a lost ship sailing the Mediterranean seas in quest of a beloved isle, and the story of a god who allows himself to be crucified on Golgatha."[30] Of course, humankind has told many more good stories. But the juxtaposition of these two illuminates a crucial difference between the secular and the sacred. The hero in the first, Odysseus, is profoundly human, an everyman locked within history. The hero in the second is the God, the ground of reality, the creator of history. Jesus deeply engaged himself in the first kind of story. Centuries of Christian dogma have evolved the second. Both kinds address human adaptation to traumatic and violent events. Jesus promoted fearlessness, dialogue, movement, and the use of one's wits to destabilize human violence in the here and now. Christian dogma, on the other hand, has domesticated violence by giving it sanctuary in a timeless divine perspective.

Almost nothing is more traumatic than an execution. The New Testament describes the disciples as very disturbed and despondent over the killing of Jesus. They were overwhelmed with fearfulness, their core positive beliefs stretched to the point of breaking (Mark 14:43-72). The disciples' background belief in a God who had covenanted to protect His people (in Jesus's time oppressed and occupied by Rome) and their probable hopes in Jesus as an apocalyptic leader were shattered. Joanna McGrath observes that their powerlessness and solitude in the face of the overwhelming mortal threat to Jesus are the precipitating conditions for post-traumatic stress disorder, which is diagnosed when a person (or, by extension, a community) responds with "intense fear, helplessness, or horror" to an event that involves "actual or threatened death or serious injury, or a threat to the physical integrity of self or others."[31]

The disciples recovered emotionally through a process of "post-traumatic growth," a group experience of "sense-making" of Jesus's execution, which allowed them to perceive it as having beneficial personal significance. Luke's report of two disciples meeting a stranger on the road to Emmaus has been identified as a "sophisticated microcosmic account" of the paradigm shift in the disciples' thinking that promoted their growth out of trauma (Luke 24:13-35). The stranger, whom the two disciples later concluded had been Jesus himself, introduced the "radical idea" that "it was necessary" for Jesus to suffer as God's Messiah.[32]

This schema regarding necessity rendered the execution of Jesus comprehensible and restored a sense of empowerment to the disciples, as they searched for emotional resiliency. The "uncontrollability of the events" around the judicial murder of Jesus was "reappraised as *apparent rather than real.* What seemed unjust and random start[ed] to be depicted as planned and just."[33] The disciples applied the super-real, the sacred, to their interpretation of the event, giving it an artificially imposed sense of moral rightness. What was subsequently understood as the benevolent and sacred sacrifice of Jesus the Christ was deemed real. The execution of Jesus the man (the gross messiness of the human legal system and the killing itself) then became an emotionally more tolerable shadow.

Taken up in church atonement dogma, the sacred story about necessity has been broadcast through centuries as a source of hope and resiliency for all Christians challenged by the sureness of pain and death in human experience. However, as a psychological denial of tragedy and an implicit endorsement of divine violence, it also has seriously hindered Christians' natural capacities for empathy. Once they had adopted the perspective of eternity, who among the early disciples protested the *beneficial* execution of Jesus? What single word of protest is there in all the New Testament? This "sense-making" of the execution gave solace, but it also began to nourish the theme of inevitable divine violence. It became a predatory story. The Apostle Paul, for example, began to articulate the necessity of the execution as appeasement of the wrath of God against humanity. But for Christ's substitution in our place, he said, we all would be facing our own homicide at God's hand (Romans 3:23-26, 5:9, 5:18; 1 Thess. 1:10, 5:9).

Atonement theology inoculates Jesus's execution from moral criticism. Extended to human punishment, the theology spins a comforting explanation of the state murder of Jesus into a violent divine mold for human events. The sacred overwhelms the secular reality and promotes violent repetition. The super-real overcomes the real. As a result, a fundamentalist theologian can confidently explain, "The concept of retributive justice is rooted in the very heart of God's character and the gospel itself. Capital punishment is actually the application on the human plane of the principle of retributive justice demonstrated by God himself in the cross of Jesus Christ."[34]

The speculative foundation of retribution as a belief is exposed here. Is God retributive and violent? What if God is not? What if this simple premise is wrong? *Jesus said it was wrong.* If we want to believe Jesus's assertions about God in the

Sermon on the Mount and in his instructions about the way his followers are to bear themselves toward *all* others, then God *cannot* be retributive. It is not possible to reconcile the apocalyptic God who executed Christ (or allowed his execution for greater ends) with *Jesus*, who says: "Do not judge, and you will not be judged. Do not condemn, and you will not be condemned. Forgive, and you will be forgiven" (Luke 6:37). Under the rule announced by Jesus (love your enemies), setting the moral scales of the universe aright through vengeance or violence is unthinkable, either as a divine or human option.

Going Beyond Predation

Immediately following the command that is implied in Jesus's prayer, that we constantly forgive others, appear the words: "*and lead us not into temptation, but deliver us from evil*" (Matt. 6:13). By this, Jesus sought to reinforce his followers' vigilant dance to avoid the cycles of violence created by predatory stories. The dance works with the two primary emotions humans have toward each other—fear and love—by transforming the former into the latter. The temptation to fall to fear and rejoin the pack is so strong that Jesus asked his disciples to pray that God would not let the gravity of the temptation to fear slow down their turning. *Forgive us as we forgive, and lead us away from failure to forgive.*

The constant presencing of the kingdom in Jesus's prayer diminishes fear of death and, as a consequence, fear of the pack. It does so because it undermines aloneness by always summoning a community—sometimes a community only as large as two. *Our* father; give *us*; forgive *us*; lead *us*. . . . It is in essence dialogical, dynamic, and bridge forming. One who prays the prayer is never alone, not simply because of the implied vertical relationship with God, but also because of the implied horizontal relationship with other(s): family, friends, strangers, enemies. The focus on summoning the kingdom grounds us with a complete trust that we are in relationship; we are essentially not alone, no matter where we go nor whom nor what we encounter.

The Jewish scholar Martin Buber once was asked what happens after death. His reply was just "that we are God's." We are in the hands of a compassionate Other, and that is all that matters. Christians may be challenged by his elaboration:

> We know nothing of death, nothing other than the one fact that we shall die—but what is that, dying? We do not know. So it behooves us to accept that it is the end of everything conceivable by us. To wish to extend our conception beyond death, to wish to anticipate in the soul what death alone can reveal to us in existence, seems to me to be a lack of faith clothed as faith.[35]

Whether or not we believe in a transcendent God, we may find that a meaningful path is offered in Jesus's wager to risk everything in compassion. This would mean always bringing oneself into the constant presence of the world's violence in such a way as to encourage dialogue and reconciliation rather than acceptance or rationalization. It would include doing the best we can to realize the peaceable kingdom within the single and wonderful life that bounds our experience now, in this day, in this moment.

Centuries of speculative doctrine ("lack of faith clothed as faith") have taken the sting out of Jesus's death and have masked its amoral brutality at the hands of the Roman regime. Present day homicidal cultures manifest similar speculative compromises of faith in the statements of their public officials.

But Jesus the strategist can be interpreted as having given us some practical suggestions for enduring and transforming that violence: (1) we remain where possible in emotionally and spiritually supportive community (at minimum, in pairs); (2) we understand that the political and spiritual powers in the world always are potentially violent; (3) we recognize the constant temptation to join the pack; (4) we approach fear by risking everything while being as strategically prescient as those who are wrapped up in violence; (5) we bring our home (the peaceable kingdom) with us; and, most importantly, (6) we remain in constant movement, summoning forgiveness and reconciliation in every moment in every encounter with others, and avoiding temptations toward deadly stasis and complacency. This is *very* hard. The gate is narrow. We know that we cross the threshold, if at all, with limited successes.

Being Compassionate Animals

Biology and culture have hardwired us for both revenge and forgiveness.[36] Surely just because revenge seems to come naturally for us does not mean that *violence* is intrinsic to our nature or to the divine. Key to human survival will be our ability to train ourselves to recognize that gross insults (such as a murder in our community), which stimulate our retributive survival instinct, can be answered and ameliorated in caring communities through legal systems adequate to protect our dignity—systems composed of adequate laws, adequate enforcement of those laws, and adequate means for restoration of those who have suffered indignities and those who have committed them.

Key also for our survival will be the development among ourselves of the wisdom that we are a biological species.

We live as vulnerable mammals bound within the uncertain dimensions of space and time. We are in profound need of verbal communication, emotional contact, touch, and warmth from others in our species. Without that human connection, we go into severe distress.[37] We are not, in essence, the isolated individuals imagined in retributive models, molded as we are by biology, environment, and our interactions with others. On subconscious levels, our bodies always are reciprocally regulated by those of others—affecting our "hormone levels, cardiovascular function, sleep rhythms, immune function, and more."[38] Science is confirming that, no matter our social station, we are all bound up inextricably in each other's neurobiology. Ultimately, our physical and emotional quality of life rises or falls with that of our neighbors *and* our enemies.

What deeply affects you affects me (or us), and vice versa. A clear example is the neurobiological effects of the attack on the World Trade Center (and our country's retributive response) upon ourselves and the citizens of the world.[39] Those actions continue to resonate throughout the legal, practical, and emotional experiences of human beings in many places. Recognizing our interconnectedness and mutual vulnerability as a species, we should create and sustain social systems that provide the greatest potential for the respect of human dignity and, consequently, the least potential for human emotional trauma.

My home state Texas has done the opposite up to now. For example, when the Texas legislature reinstated the death penalty in 1973, the lawmakers conducted no inquiry whatsoever into the traumatic effects that the death penalty had (and would have) on people living in Texas. During House floor debate immediately before the bill's passage, the author of the legislation defended his bill by quoting Genesis and other parts of the Torah, asserting that the murderer's shed blood always would cleanse the land of the defilement caused by the crime. He was joined by other representatives arguing from similar passages, which finally prompted one of the opponents to stand and ask the house speaker if he was aware that the proponents, "being . . . Baptist, only quote[d] Mosaic law?"[40]

The death penalty in Texas is only one of many indications of a culture that is "trauma organized." Instead of acting in proactive ways to reduce trauma, Texas government tends to be reactive, addressing traumatic situations with trauma-inducing solutions.[41] Texas's punitive criminal justice system, informed by a culture of excessive individualism and Christian fundamentalism, feeds a cycle of violence that begins with a neglect of human needs across the board. Texas is at the bottom of the list of states in providing for the necessities of children though such services as health care, mental health care, prenatal care, pre-school programs, child care, and education. Because of its legislative priorities, Texas fails to solve its huge problems with school dropout rates, teen pregnancy, and juvenile crime. It then reacts punitively to these and other problems, spending three times as much money to house each state prisoner as it does to support each school student.[42]

On a societal level, we need to learn to resist the temptation to react with instinctive retribution and then rationalize our harsh actions with a "righteousness behind the suffering." We need to listen deeply to human needs, understanding that vengeance responds to outrages committed against dignity. The retributive urge is natural, perhaps innate. But we must mindfully endeavor to prevent it from becoming violent policy. In part that means aggressively pursuing the elimination of poverty, inadequate education, inadequate health care, and inadequate provision of treatment and support for persons traumatized by violence, which are themselves outrages against dignity.

I labor under the impression that my religion is a cause of deep suffering as it nurtures America's last bastion of capital punishment. Over the years, this impression has challenged my ability to find spiritual refuge from the emotional trauma I have incurred in my job. The shame it induces has caused me to ask whether, indeed, there is anything worth retaining in my religion. Throughout, however, I have prayed the Lord's Prayer, and as I have reflected on that experience, I have realized that the prayer has helped me to keep from coming apart at the seams. It has helped me retain some equanimity. For the most part, I have not become lost in anger or despair and, when faced with circumstances that have seemed like crucifixions, I have kept moving. Movement is critical. The lightness of forgiveness is essential, in part because there is no authentic sense-making of an execution. At the same time that I can report some resiliency in trying to follow Jesus's strategy, I confess that I live in fear. With Texas's incessant killing, I am triggered almost daily to recall past execution traumas.

Fearless compassion speaks to the bestial tendencies within all of us on behalf of dignity—our own, our neighbor's, our enemy's dignity. Refuge in Jesus is not a place or a state; it is not necessarily survival in the ordinary or supernatural senses. It is *doing*, caring movement among others undergirded by pursuit of forgiveness at every turn. It is, thus, living in the kingdom. As Jesus said in the parable of the Good Samaritan, it is *being mercy*. In principle, the distance between neighbor and enemy has been dissolved. In fact, each act of self-forgiveness and forgiveness of others is a small resurrection—a revivifying contact with others—and a source of hope for a less violent, more just future.

Endnotes

1. Christina M. Cerna, "Universality of Human Rights: The Case of the Death Penalty," *ILSA Journal of International and Comparative Law* 3 (1997): 465, 475 ("[T]he imposition of the death penalty itself is the most extreme form of torture imaginable, but is excluded from the definition of torture by means of a legal fiction.") Cerna wrote as a senior specialist in human rights at the Inter-American Commission on Human Rights of the Organization of American States.
2. Evaluating Caiaphas' role as Jesus' prosecutor, a Texas law professor (and ex-prosecutor) has observed, "Perhaps as we celebrate the passion of Christ, we should also see the tragic passions of the prosecutor and recognize the shadowy dangers they create." Mark Osler, *Jesus on Death Row: The Trial of Jesus and American Capital Punishment* (Nashville: Abingdon Press, 2009), 86.
3. All American death penalty states are caught in the same ethically challenged web of federal and state laws that, by design, press the courts to move cases toward execution. Bad decisions are produced everywhere, but Texas courts tend to receive more criticism because the state's aggressive prosecution drives them to be more active. The following decisions are by Texas's highest court in death row inmates' cases (from the most recent, 2009, to the oldest, 1995): 1) Charles Hood (the court denied relief after it was proven that the trial prosecutor and judge were having a sexual affair during the trial); 2) Scott Panetti (the court denied relief to a schizophrenic man who acted as his own attorney at trial in a "bizarre," "scary," and "trance-like" state); 3) Gary Graham (the court denied an evidentiary hearing on evidence from two disinterested eyewitnesses that contradicted the State's lone eyewitness description of the perpetrator); 4) Cesar Fierro (the court changed its harm standard in denying relief to a defendant who had proven that a police officer committed perjury to cover up extremely coercive techniques used to get his confession); and 5) Calvin Burdine (the court denied relief even though it had been proven that the sole defense attorney slept while the prosecutor questioned witnesses and presented evidence).

4. All Bible quotations are from the New International Version, unless otherwise noted.
5. Blaise Pascal, *Pensees* (Indianapolis: Hackett, 2005), 212–213.
6. Addressing atonement doctrine, Leo Tolstoy argued that it is impossible to reconcile a God who "cursed the human race and . . . doomed his son to be a victim, and . . . doomed a part of humanity to everlasting torment" with "a God of love." Simultaneously, he observed that belief in the "doctrine and preaching of the church about the compatibility of executions and wars with Christianity" is flatly incompatible with Jesus's moral imperative to love. Tolstoy concluded that belief in creeds causes the Sermon on the Mount to become superfluous. Following the Sermon on the Mount, on the other hand, causes creeds, churches, and representatives of churches to lose significance. Leo Tolstoy, *The Kingdom of God Is Within You* (New York: Farrar, Straus, and Giroux, 1961), 79, 87.
7. See David Boulton, *Who on Earth Was Jesus? The Modern Quest for the Jesus of History* (Hants, United Kingdom: O Books, 2008), 380–381.
8. "There is an accusation against Jews and Judaism in the New Testament that has done incalculable harm: 'You have heard it said, "You shall love your neighbor and hate your enemy." But I say to you, "Love your enemy also."' Nowhere in the Pentateuch [Torah] does it say, 'Hate your enemy.'" Lord Jonathan Sacks, *Helping An Enemy,* The Jewish Press, February 10, 2010 (online at: http://www.jewishpress.com/pageroute.do/42510). (Sacks is the chief rabbi of the United Hebrew Congregations of the British Commonwealth.)
9. Ibid.
10. Quoted in James J. Megivern, *The Death Penalty: An Historical and Theological Survey* (Mahwah, NJ: Paulist Press, 1997), 20.
11. Augustine of Hippo, *The City of God* (New York: Doubleday Image, 1958), I: 21:57. "Since the agent of authority is but a sword in the hand, and is not responsible for the killing, it is in no way contrary to the commandment, 'Thou shalt not kill,' to wage war at God's bidding, or . . . to put criminals to death" (ca. 410 CE).
12. "Penal substitution" seems to be the prevailing view in Texas churches, which are strongly influenced by the Calvinist tradition. John Calvin,

a lawyer, maintained that God made Jesus "a sponsor and surety for the guilty, and, as it were, subjected to condemnation, [paying] all the penalties which must have been exacted from [humanity], the only exception being that the pains of death could not hold him." John Calvin, *Institutes of the Christian Religion* (Grand Rapids: Eerdmans Publishing Co., 1990), book 2, ch. 16, para. 10.

13. Gustav Aulen, *Christus Victor: An Historical Study of the Three Main Types of the Idea of the Atonement* (New York: Macmillan, 1977).
14. See J. Denny Weaver, *The Nonviolent Atonement* (Cambridge, England: Eerdmans, 2001) for a good survey of atonement doctrines and their practical effects and a Mennonite's attempt to articulate a nonviolent version.
15. Lynn Hunt describes the process that peaked in the discovery of bodily integrity and empathetic selfhood in the last half of the eighteenth century: "The constant evolution of notions of interiority and depth of psyche from the Christian soul to the Protestant conscience to the eighteenth-century notions of sensibility filled the self with new content. . . . Torture as part of the judicial process and the most extreme forms of corporal punishment both came to be seen as unacceptable. All of these changes contributed to a sense of the separation and self-possession of individual bodies, along with the possibility of empathy with others." *Inventing Human Rights: A History* (New York: Norton 2008), 30.
16. Following the Italian jurist Cesare Beccaria, the English jurist William Blackstone captured the Enlightenment view, which incorporated empathy into the criminal law as follows: [The law should always be] "conformable to the dictates of truth and justice, the *feelings of humanity,* and the indelible rights of mankind." *Commentaries on the Law of England* (Oxford: Clarendon Press, 1778), vol. 4, no. 3, quoted in Hunt, supra, 81 (emphasis added).
17. Benjamin Rush, "An Enquiry into the Effects of Public Punishments upon Criminals, and Upon Society, Read in the Society for Promoting Political Enquiries, Convened at the House of His Excellency Benjamin Franklin, Esquire, in Philadelphia, March 9, 1787" (Philadelphia: Joseph James 1787) in *Reform of Criminal Law*

in Pennsylvania: Selected Enquiries, 1787-1810 (New York: Arno Press, 1972), 6–7, 13, quoted in Hunt, supra, 109.

18. See, for example, *Universal Declaration of Human Rights*, Preamble: "Whereas recognition of the inherent dignity and of the equal and inalienable rights of all members of the human family is the foundation of freedom, justice and peace in the world. . . ." (The Declaration was adopted by the United Nations in 1948.)
19. Constitutional Court of Germany, *The Microcensus Case*, 27 BverfGE 1 (holding that "the state violates human dignity when it treats persons as mere objects").
20. *Furman v. Georgia*, 408 U.S. 238, 272–73 (1972) (Brennan, J., concurring).
21. *Kindler v. Canada*, 6 CRR (2d) 193, 241 (SC) (1992) (Cory, J.); see also *State v. Makwanyane*, Case No. CCT/3/94, 1995(3) SA 391 (CC) (S.Afr.).
22. *EU Policy on the Death Penalty*, Brussels, July 14, 2003, 11249/03 (Presse 204), 83/03 (declaration by the presidency of the European Union: "[T]he death penalty in all circumstances . . . impairs the human dignity").
23. *The State v. Makwanyane*, supra, para. 232. "Society cannot now succumb to the doctrine of an eye for an eye."
24. See Howard Thurman, *Jesus and the Disinherited* (Boston: Beacon Press, 1976), 33: "Jesus . . . was not protected by the normal guarantees of citizenship—that quiet sense of security which comes from knowing that you belong and the general climate of confidence which it inspires." Also see Martin Luther King, Jr., "Letter from Birmingham City Jail" in James W. Washington, ed., *A Testament of Hope: The Essential Writings and Speeches of Martin Luther King, Jr.* (San Francisco: Harper, 1986), 292–293:"[W]hen you are forever fighting a degenerating sense of 'nobodiness' . . . then you will understand why we find it difficult to wait."
25. "But when you give to the needy, do not let your right hand know what your left hand is doing" (Matt. 6:3). In the opening verses of the sixth chapter of Matthew, Jesus instructed his disciples to deftly sidestep their pretentions (and their corresponding narcissistic anxi-

ety about themselves) as preparation for seeking genuine contact with others through their practice of the Lord's Prayer.

26. Dorothee Soelle, *Suffering* (Philadelphia: Fortress Press, 1975), 32.
27. See Daniel A. Cohen, *Pillars of Salt, Monuments of Grace: New England Crime Literature and the Origins of American Popular Culture, 1674-1860* (Boston: University of Massachusetts Press, 2006); Lloyd Steffen, *Executing Justice: The Moral Meaning of the Death Penalty* (Cleveland: Pilgrim Press, 1998).
28. Tony Karnes, "The Burning Bush from Texas," *Christianity Today,* October 2, 2000 (quoting George W. Bush).
29. Individual physicians might in good faith believe that their assistance in executions would be compassionate, because they could reduce the potential that the inmate would feel excruciating pain in the execution process. However, as the American Medical Association and other such organizations have found, such assistance is "doing harm" in violation of the doctors' Hippocratic Oath. The American Board of Anesthesiologists recently decided to revoke the certification of any member who participates in lethal injection. The Board secretary stated that this reflected the Board's belief that doctors were "healers, not executioners" (Rob Stein, "Group to Censure Physicians Who Play Role in Lethal Injections," *Washington Post,* May 2, 2010, A1). A state prison chaplain's decision to stand by a condemned man and perhaps reach out and touch his leg to give him a sense of human connection as his veins are filled with poison equally mistakes pity for compassion. Despite the silence of denominational ethics committees, this is "doing harm." This is participation in a homicide.
30. Jorge Luis Borges, "The Gospel According to Mark," in *Collected Fictions* (New York: Penguin, 1998), 400.
31. Joanna Collicutt McGrath, "Post-Traumatic Growth and the Origins of Early Christianity," *Mental Health, Religion and Culture,* vol. 9, no. 3 (2006): 294 (quoting the *Diagnostic and Statistical Manual of Mental Disorders,* 4th ed., criteria for PTSD).
32. McGrath, supra, 301.
33. Ibid (emphasis added).

34. John Jefferson Davis, *Evangelical Ethics: Issues Facing the Church Today* (Phillipsburg, New Jersey: P and R Publishing, 2004), 214.
35. Martin Buber, "After Death" in *A Believing Humanism: Gleanings by Martin Buber,* Ruth Nanda Anshen, ed. (New York: Simon and Schuster, 1969), 231.
36. Social scientists have posited that the American South's widespread and uniquely strong attitudes about punishment—represented, for example, in criminal laws enforcing strict punishments (including the death penalty) and in school and family laws preserving corporal punishment of children—may represent evolutionary adaptations to circumstances that have long ceased to exist. Michael E. McCullough, *Beyond Revenge: The Evolution of the Forgiveness Instinct* (San Francisco: Jossey-Bass, 2008), 52–54, 232; Aaron T. Beck, M.D., *Prisoners of Hate: The Cognitive Basis of Anger, Hostility, and Violence* (New York: Harper Collins, 1999), 164–166.
37. "The mammalian nervous system depends for its neurophysiologic stability on a system of interactive coordination, wherein steadiness comes from synchronization with nearby attachment figures. Protest is the alarm that follows a breach of these life-sustaining adjustments. If the interruption continues, physiologic rhythms decline into the painful unruliness of despair," and sometimes death. Thomas Lewis, Fari Amini, and Richard Lannon, *A General Theory of Love* (New York: Vintage, 2000), 84. "Cortisol is the body's major stress hormone, and its sharp elevation in separated mammals tells us that relationship rupture is a severe bodily strain," pp. 77–78.
38. Ibid., 85.
39. See Sandra Bloom, "Neither Liberty Nor Safety: The Impact of Fear on Individuals, Institutions, and Societies," published in four parts in *Psychotherapy and Politics International,* vol. 2, no. 2 (2004): 78-98; vol. 2, no. 3 (2004): 212-28; vol. 3, no. 2 (2005): 96-111; and vol. 4, no. 1 (2006): 4-23.
40. Floor debate, Texas House of Representatives, House Bill 200, May 10, 1973, 63rd Legislature (unpublished transcript in files of the author). Representative Craig Washington's appeal to the speaker simultaneously exposed selective Christian use of Jewish scriptures to

endorse violent goals and what I find to be an Establishment Clause violation. See *Edwards v. Aguillard,* 482 U.S. 578, 585 (1987): "A governmental intention to promote religion is clear when the State enacts a law to serve a religious purpose." Such "intention may be evidenced by . . . advancement of a particular religious belief."

41. "Trauma and its immediate and long-term effects have become a central organizing principle for [the] entire social structure." Sandra L. Bloom and Michael Reichert, *Bearing Witness: Violence and Collective Responsibility* (New York: Haworth Maltreatment and Trauma Press, 1998), 14.
42. National Education Association, *Rankings and Estimates: A Report of School Statistics Update* (Fall 2005): $7,142.00/year; and National Association of State Budget Officers, *2003 State Expenditures Report* (http://www.nasbo.org/Publications/PDFs/2003ExpendReport.pdf): $20,232.00/year.

Discussion Questions

1. What does it mean to you to "love your enemies and pray for those who persecute you" (Matt. 5:44)? How have you sought to do this in your life? If you have been changed by this practice, describe your experience.
2. Who is the true "neighbor"?
3. Central to the author's faith is the passage from the Lord's Prayer: "Forgive us as we forgive those who trespass against us." Describe a situation from your own life when you forgave someone. What was difficult? How do you feel about this experience today?
4. How does the "Lord's Prayer" produce "*revivifying* human attachment" (p. 5)?
5. How do you respond to the author's contention that Christian atonement theories "present God as an agent of Jesus's death

and describe the death itself as a benefit of ultimate value for the believer"? (See p. 12.) According to the author, what impact can acceptance of such atonement theories have on a person's response to suffering and sense of responsibility for violence in the world? Do you agree? Why or why not?

6. In light of Martin Buber's comments about death and faith (on p. 24), what relation, if any, do you think that Christian belief in an afterlife has to tolerance of the death penalty?

7. What does "dignity" mean to you?

8. How would you describe "an art of small resurrections" in your own words? (On p. 17 the author writes, "It is the incessant bringing to life of relationships through constant, momentary repentance: the cessation of *judgment* and simultaneously . . . the ending of violence.")

9. How do you respond to Dorothee Soelle's statement (on p. 18), "In the face of suffering you are either with the victim or the executioner—there is no other option"?

10. How does the author believe that Jesus's execution was made comprehensible to his followers?

11. The author writes: "Atonement theology inoculates Jesus's execution from moral criticism" and can lead to the belief that "the concept of retributive justice is rooted in the very heart of God's character and the gospel itself" (p. 22). How do you respond?

12. The author writes that presencing of the kingdom diminishes fear of the "pack" by summoning "community" (p. 23). What are the differences between "the pack" and "community" for humans? How broad or thin is the border between them?

13. What practical suggestions does the author say that Jesus gives us for living compassionately and enduring and transforming violence?